Extremely Lightweight Guns

Extremely Lightweight Guns

poems

Nikki Moustaki

Red Hen Press | *Pasadena, CA*

Book design by Mark E. Cull

Library of Congress Cataloging-in-Publication Data

Names: Moustaki, Nikki, 1970– author.
Title: Extremely lightweight guns : poems / Nikki Moustaki.
Description: First edition. | Pasadena, CA : Red Hen Press, [2021]
Identifiers: LCCN 2020037248 (print) | LCCN 2020037249 (ebook) | ISBN
    9781597091138 (trade paperback) | ISBN 9781597094658 (epub)
Subjects: LCGFT: Poetry.
Classification: LCC PS3613.O879 E98 2021 (print) | LCC PS3613.O879
    (ebook) | DDC 811/.6—dc23
LC record available at https://lccn.loc.gov/2020037248
LC ebook record available at https://lccn.loc.gov/2020037249

The National Endowment for the Arts, the Los Angeles County Arts Commission, the Ahmanson Foundation, the Dwight Stuart Youth Fund, the Max Factor Family Foundation, the Pasadena Tournament of Roses Foundation, the Pasadena Arts & Culture Commission and the City of Pasadena Cultural Affairs Division, the City of Los Angeles Department of Cultural Affairs, the Audrey & Sydney Irmas Charitable Foundation, the Kinder Morgan Foundation, the Meta & George Rosenberg Foundation, the Albert and Elaine Borchard Foundation, the Adams Family Foundation, the Riordan Foundation, Amazon Literary Partnership, the Sam Francis Foundation, and the Mara W. Breech Foundation partially support Red Hen Press.

First Edition
Published by Red Hen Press
www.redhen.org

Acknowledgments

Grateful acknowledgment is made to the editors of the following publications in which these poems first appeared:

An earlier version of "Here's a Pill" appeared in *The Complete Idiot's Guide to Writing Poetry*; Sections of "Dreaming of Chickens" have appeared in *Cream City Review*; *Madison Review*, "Planned Disappearances," "The Incubator," "The Mind's Negatives"; and *Slope*, "Extremely Lightweight Guns."

Thank you to the National Endowment of the Arts for the grant that helped make this manuscript possible.

Contents

Extremely Lightweight Guns

I

THE MIND'S NEGATIVES

I leave the thing a problem, like all things.
—Lord Byron

1. [The Woman]

I don't remember what I screamed.
A word with few syllables. Maybe I didn't open
my mouth at all, the scream, my shirt's collar ripping
in his palm, concrete stairs, one flight, another, elbows
and knees wrapping each stair red

until a neighbor emerged from an apartment across the corridor
and I ducked into the neighbor's place,
locked the door, hearing *him* complain outside,
I don't know what's wrong with her, little knuckles
on the door, voice sweet, pleading, *come out, my love.*

It was summer. The neighbor's apartment was cool, tan carpet
stained here and there with dog, snub-nosed Boxer staring up at me,
cropped tail wiggling, licking my bloodied knees.
The neighbor's caged parakeet on the dinette. A row
of glass beakers displayed on a shelf—
and I startled at my reflection in the smoked mirror above the bar—

I am not this woman, I thought. *This is not my life.*
The woman in the mirror tasted the temperature drop in there.
The trickle of blood—*her blood*—into her socks,
the dog's muzzle, the underbite, and out the window
red and blue lights, the knocking faster, *please,*
I don't want to go to jail again, and her twisting the lock,
ashamed of her blood—*her blood!*—ashamed of the fall, the stairs.

You have to tell your mother, the woman in the mirror told him,
so they drove an hour to his mother's place and his mother asked her:

What did you say to make him do this?
Examining the elbows and knees, offering them
a bed the woman forgot to make in the morning,
and him, later: *You're rude for not folding the sheets.*

Back at their place, they patched the walls with posters
of worn mountains and placid seas, so many posters
and an unmatching door, spackle in various states of drying,
the construction of so many *I'm leaving*s and *You're not going*s
singing in her head, and Band-Aids on her knees.

2. [The Stairs]

Inside the hand: the push, the palm, the shoulder's
blades, the stairs, the tumble, neighbors and police.
Inside the hand: the body of the push, falling stairs.
Inside the hand: the body, pushed. Inside the hand:
the shrieking bird, sirens, the fruit and pulp of ache.

Inside the palm: the body of the hand, the giving
and the taking-back, the push behind the push, stairs,
the bottom of the stairs, wailing bird, police.
Inside the palm: detainment. Inside the palm: release.
Inside the palm: the cup and lines of disbelief.

Inside the fingers: flame. A storm's five eyes, the give
and not the take. The fingers clench inside the palm,
the palm a fist, the fist a wall, the wall the skin wrapped
around a house that screams without a mouth, the mouth
a fist in the woman's teeth. The phone call. Finally. Police.

3. [The Woman]

Why did the holes in the walls not seem like tunnels out of there?
I kept sneakers by the door
so white I could return them to the store.
Why did my feet go numb when he raised his hands?

The holes scream when he whimpers.
He paces, his guilt-walking wearing a strip in the carpet.

Shoes by the door.
Where are my feet? Where are my hands?
I am not this woman. This is not my life.

An hour to sunrise, beneath pink cotton sheets,
he snores the sleep of the blessed.

It won't matter that my mind's negatives
will have to be burned someday.

In the walls, memory sits like bruises hidden beneath shirtsleeves.

I am the inventor of silence.

Inside the push, the heart's atoms, such bits of advice for the body:

You will know the stairs as well as you know your own knees.
You will dream his hands inside you when you sleep.

4. [The Stairs]

Inside the house: the hand, the fist, the silent mouth,
the stairs, the push. Hand set firm between the blades,
shoulders firm between the body, body falling firm
between the walls, inside the walls the scream, inside
the scream, police. Inside their car the hands release.

Inside the hand: the calcium of push. Inside the push:
the rage between the palm and blades, shoulders'
gentle, downward grace. Inside the tumble: knees
on stairs, blood on knees, the "accidental" push, police.
Inside the push: report, the lie, arrest, release.

Inside the house: the sorry, screaming. Inside the sorry:
the phosphorous of belief. The hand unclenched.
The sleeping bird. The fist and fingers, released.
The stairs are cleaned. The neighbors calmed, the house,
the scream, the walls, the stairs, the knees, palm, police.

5. [The Blackbird Woman]

Once there was a woman.
No one loved the woman and the woman grew blind.

She couldn't see the blackbirds perched in her belly like tumors
waiting to turn into hands and choke her.

No one could see the blackbirds either, so they grew until the woman
herself turned into a blackbird shaped like a woman.

You could look through her into a world where no one had hands,
just wings that cut the air like a juggler's knives.

The woman walked around with her wings
because no one told her she could fly.

She assumed she was merely a lens
through which others hated themselves.

Their faces transformed in her, became feral and mean.
The woman absolved herself daily with suicide,

but every morning she'd wake, unfurl her oily wings, and step
into day where people ignored her.

But this isn't about how the woman learned to fly,
because she didn't.

This is about how, even as sorrow eddies around her
like the moonlight she tries to see, even as her eyes dim

and her wings begin painful molting, even as she
is hated for her ignorance, it is she that is remembered.

6. [Cento: The Poet]

There was a time when, though my path was rough,
I'd wake and hear the cold splintering, breaking,
reflected from the snow by the bright spring sun
where perhaps some beauty lies—
I had only begun to know the kind of pain others endure—
they represented, I fancied, a version of heaven.

This morning as I walked out of your room,
I stood by the bed of a girl, or the frayed knee
slowly risen in the night to overflow
all time, amid the ruins of ancient chaos
in a poem that won't quite fit, giving it wrong
like dirty words rubbed off a slate.

What I took in my hand
glowed into words, then would be savagely still.
I have been stupid in a poem:
of detail, burned, dissolved, and broken off
like the ghost of a snowfield in summer.

Into the rain-washed evening white with evangelical fury,
noticed but unknown, a sleepwalker afraid of the dark,
walking with no purpose past buildings that would stand forever.
I think we must give up something, or stop something, or maybe look—

Where the beautiful mingles with the common, it is the beautiful that suffers.

7. [The Woman]

He overturned the fish tank, three goldfish skidding
in a tsunami of gravel and glass—

next the oven tipped on its mouth, cups
shattered, plates smashed, cupboards off their hinges.

The couch turned legs-up. Chairs off their feet.

I am not this woman.

The television's face
kicked into a gape
so black you could see death in there.

This is not my life.

Bathroom mirror shattered:
seven years more of this,
our shower head knocked free, water streaming—

Then *my* hands opened and his face *slapped*.

My hands
ripping the shower curtain from its hooks,
my hands
tearing our anniversary photograph,
my hands
foreign from the wrist down.

The push belonged to me, too.

He held me down.
I cried *rape*.

Rape, again, I yelled to the destroyed home,
to my fish drying on the hardwood floor.

I liked the sound—*rape*—
and his face became the vision of composure.

I could push too.

You want me to go to jail? he asked.
For starters, I said, *I want you to bake me a pie—*

8. [The Blackbird Woman]

One day the congregation found the woman after a great wind had blown
her onto the roof of their church, wings spread wide, awaiting something.

Some people thought she was a bad omen,
marking the church for fire or a death in the pews.

Some thought she was a vision and fell to their knees,
ruining their yellow Sunday dresses.

Some thought she should be removed, so they removed her,
but they couldn't fold her wings into her body.

There she stood, outside the church, wings wide,
wind shuffling the feathers like cards,

which made the ladies remember their bridge game
and they went off whispering.

The sound made the fellows remember their hunting trip,
and they strolled away smacking each other on their backs.

The woman folded her wings and began walking home,
which wasn't her home at all, but the place where she lived.

The greatest of all possibilities is that she never makes it home.
After all, it's a long way after such a great wind.

9. [The Woman]

—I want rhubarb and cherry and lots of sugar in the pie.
I want sugar and butter and graham crackers and blood in the crust.

I want it sweet, very sweet. I want diabetic coma from this pie,
because I am not this woman and this is not my life.

Then I want you to call the police and tell them
what you did to the fish,

and I want you to serve them the pie, and I want you
to call your mother and ask her for money for a truck

to move all my stuff, yes, even the broken television,
then I want you to choke on the fucking pie,

and I will be very quiet, like I wasn't even here—

10. [Cento: The Poet]

A woman is dragging her shadow in a circle:
I cannot rub that strangeness from my sight—
Once you, a woman, came

and paced above the mountains overhead,
like several boxes in descending sizes, one above the other,
there, among sunflowers, goldenrod, and thistle,
as blazed from story into history,
uttering cries that are almost human.

I slept last night under a bird's shadow—
I knew how to lift myself through the air,
returning before sunrise, stepping in the moonlight—

I know you are reading this poem
in a clumsy way, where much more is moving
and nothing quite so least as truth
rises off the bones.

What answer does it signal? And who are you
in a poem that won't quite fit, giving the wrong
Marvelous Truth, confronting us—
I will show you fear in a handful of dust.

If the shoe fell from the other foot, who would hear?
I answer that I cannot answer. You must find out for yourself.

11. [The Woman]

—*then I will do unspeakable things to your body.*

I will tell the police I have never seen you before.

They will find the pie in your throat and black
birds in your belly, and believe you were a king.

They will find bits of me beneath your nails.

I will lie and say you put them there.

They will believe me.

I will finish the pie and then haul you to the stairwell.
I will tell people along the way that a blackbird woman
on the roof frightened me once,
and I believe she still lives up there.

I won't tell them that I think she's me.

They'll find one of us broken at the bottom of the stairs
like a bird shattered into a thousand wings.

II

DREAMING OF CHICKENS

Sunday: All our men are dead.

Mother's body full of nicotine and lead, she smokes
Camels and kingfish in the yard.

A cock springs upon the chickens like a hammer.

Grandmother's black-holing
the earth with her old earth-pick.

Bury the names of the dead and the sick.

From the holly the cock declares
hallelujah, hallelu-eye-ay in his silvercock,

come-hither-chicken way. Nobody brought
him here: iridescent feathers

and copper mane, razors on his bronzy dino-feet,
he shreds the chickens to chicken meat.

Mother can't catch him. Grandmother can't catch him.

We can't sell all these chicks or all these chicken bones,
all this cracked calcium mown

under with Grandmother's mature
manual mower, 1956.

Mother invites the third child from every house
in the neighborhood for chicken fricassee.

Grandmother's afraid frogs are next,
duct tapes over every orifice in the house.

The cock comes
full on into evening like a misset clock.

The neighbors are all having suicide dreams.

All our men are dead and cigarettes are free.
Death is a priority.

Grandmother doesn't close her superstition-holes
anymore, children get snared in them and sink.

There's a nicotinic halo in the stained glass lamplight
over Grandmother's genuine

nickel, fiftieth anniversary plate.
Mother waves the nimbus off like advice.

The chickens gorge on salt and chickenweed.

The neighbors' children have more children,
come knocking at our door, two by two by two by three.

Grandmother sells the poison chickens
to four-sins-or-more ladies from the Ladies' Rotary.

Today Earth hangs 91.4 million miles from the sun.

Saturn stationary. No one laughs.

Grandmother listens to each egg
before she smacks it against her aluminum bowl—

barely fertilized go to the white cake she's baking
for tonight's partial lunar eclipse.

The bloody almost-chickens
kicking in their translucent sacs go into the stew.

Lots of calcium in the unborn, Grandmother
says, stirring writhing blood and bone into tonight's dinner.

Mother comes in with a carton of menthols
and another death threat.

We must become all the men that are missing.

Mother drives me to the locked
psych ward west of downtown, signs me in, and leaves.

I brownout during lunar events.
Last time Grandmother almost lost a finger.

There's new violet carpet now. The turkey's still thin and green,
plastered with fake cranberry goo.

Pale turkey bones mean frost or gall stones.

All the apple juice you can drink.
One cigarette an hour, though whining gets you more.
A cigarette lighter on a string.

At four, a walk on the walled terrace,
the whole town spread in squares, perfect green,

as if a delicate knife cared
for this cake like a daughter's birthday.

I want to stick my finger
between the two churches, slide it up the interstate, lick.

At ten they lock me in the room next to the nurse's station.

I wake with the half-moon itching my spine, sweating,
night calling like a siren:

I will come into the possession of secrets:
Mother struggles to put forth the appearance of happiness:
Grandmother desires a journey:

    I will never marry.

Because it's Saturday,
Grandmother retrieves me
from the mental ward in her toothpaste-blue
Chevy Nova,

cigarette filters rolling in the foot-wells
like excised tumors.
She unwraps a wedge of cake
from wrinkled foil,

eyeing my first bite from behind
the knitted steering wheel cover—
to Grandmother, baking's more sacred
than secrets and death.

Inside the cake she's placed wishes,
written with burnt
kitchen matches on onion paper—

I get: Dream of a Tooth Being Filled.

Today Mother's placing green bottles
in the recycling bin as if they were gems
stacked in a glass basket.

They roll against one another like lovers
as she totes them to the curb.

I see where my body will mimic hers.

Our lawn isn't grass anymore, but river rock
studded with prickly pear.

Something will sting us this year
and it won't be me.

Each day I grow older, I grind Mother into a relic.
In each granule, Grandmother's silhouette.

The sky today is a martyr.

The chickens belly-up in the coop,
cooling their scaly feet.

If it rained rocks, sulfur, and ash,
we wouldn't turn off the fans.

It's not the heat, but love that pulverizes
everything to sand.

Grandmother's barefoot, first time in years.
Her feet are soft as grieving faces.

The house's latex paint screams
and releases the wall with a bubbling *thawp*.

Mary, give me a glass of ice water in Hell,
Grandmother says.

The Virgin won't help her today.
We all know spirits don't help for swelter.

　　The sky isn't a martyr, it's a suicide.

Mother places green glass stones
under each heat-floppy, hissing hen.

　　Green against egg binding.

It's Sunday and we're incommunicado again.

　　The sky's green face has duct tape over its mouth.

Grandmother says the bird of misfortune eats
at our table and we don't even know it.

The sky is a furious green bird whose hatchlings
are taken by a furious green snake.

We set the table with Sunday
chinaware, extra plates for our dead.

We each pray, silent, and Mother stares
at the ceiling like a lens through which she can see them.

I see them too, helpless floaters
waiting for us to release them.

We fill our stomachs,
spoons singing in our shallow bowls.

Grandmother's eating with the conviction of a brain tumor—
if she sees the dead on Sunday, she ignores them.

Monday: Grandmother claims killing
wasn't always this way.

She trumbles through the Rhode Island Reds,
plucks a porky chicken from its brethren,

spins its neck, ruddy feathers spiraling,
weighs it on the bloody scale—eleven pounds—
the heftiest chickens in town.

She sets the rigormorting hen on the cutting rock,
hacks its head plain off,

face beak-up in the grass—
the way curiosity would look shocked.

She bleeds the round neck-hole,
slings away the head,

offs the feet with shears,
and starts a pot to boil.

Mother's cruising up the driveway,
the house full with women now,

the sun skidding to dusk,
arcing to the world's other half.

Birds awake, birds asleep. Matriarchy.

Tuesday: We read from the old King James,
Arching our backs from bad mattresses

and nightmares, the old hideaway
couched now,

Grandmother changing all the *hes* to *shes,*
the biblical hierarchy

replaced with Grandmother's new-millennium
optimism: Patriarchy, here, is dead.

Our cock crows, again, again.

Mother's throwing bones, reading stones
and translating runes, tiny skeletons arcing

in her burnt copper bowl like osteoporosis;
she stirs with fingers arched like an organist.

Grandmother prays:
She is the Stone the builders rejected,
She is the Rock-of-Offense
to the unbelieving
who stumble at the Word—
the Sleeping Rock,
the Stone-a-Stumbling,
the Singing Rock,
the Matriarchical Stone,
the Birthing Rock,
the Throwing Rock,
the Killing Stone.
She-the-Architect-of-Dreams,
give us this night our daily dose.

    Amen.

Morning: Cold leftovers and a prayer
to the weatherman for more rain

and less ache in Grandmother's
knuckles, arched like a McDonald's sign.

She's got rheumatoid and the Holy Spirit
on Wednesdays
when it's freezing in the Holy Land.

We're in good spirits,
stroll to the waterway where Mother

renews her obsidian in the brine:
good for letting go of old love.

Mother and I strip and dive.

       Water for centralization.

Grandmother opens her bag of stones:
garnet for circulation,

hematite for blood,
opal for intuition, harmony, joy.

She places the gems against her chest,
bows to the Earth's four corners,
and rocks against the yellow sky:

yellow for energy, blue for oration,
white for healing,
orange for calm, blackbirds for pain,
chickens for change.

Thursday: Mother builds a limestone wall
arching around the coop.

    Coop for inner peace.

In this pre-Archean heat,
every eyeball aches for shade,

wild daisies crouch
behind rocks trying to crawl inside like water.

    Daisies for meditation.

There are bird trackways
leading toward the house—

the chickens trundle through the living room
where Grandmother's pitching rocks into a bucket,
ignoring the renegade broilers and fryers.

    Chickens for toxicity.

Mother sweeps the chickens with a rake
and checks for chicken droppings in her dainties.

Grandmother does her killing business by the coop.
The sky rocks, then falls. Nobody screams.

Day won't close without a pot
chickening on the stove.

We sleep refreshed, less one chicken,
full on breasts and thighs, love, and wanting more.

    Amen.

On Fridays Grandmother's atheist,
flings the Bible
far as she can with arthritic hands—

Killing isn't easy, she screams.
There's no Divinity, not even for chickens.

The moon arches over Friday like a killer,
silent as a nightworm.

     Worm for transformation.

The Milky Way covers the sky like a sneeze.
Grandmother's sleeping like a castaway.

     Our hens tremble in the yard.

In the kitchen hacking chicken,
Mother's cleaver has never been sharper.

She adds wine to the simmer and romances
the reds together.

The hen stipples up plum, like sandpaper
as Mother rubs the flour in.

The oven drags the kitchen into summer.
The bird rusts. Our plates deepen.

No matter the year, the chicken never changes.

What's dead remains dead.
Mother chops the bacon in.

Dusk: No one's watching the moon
tonight, tracing the sky like a train,

a flattened nickel, as the sun's shadow
settles onto its matronly face.

I call the moon out like a lost chicken
scratching its white arc against the sky,

and it clucks back—
the wind has changed again.

We move the couch back from the window,
point our beds' heads North.

Mother slips amber chips beneath our pillows
for mental precision and female vigor,
sets leeches on my back as the frightened
moon calls me like a dead sister—

She needs the sun,
she hates the sun,
shifting its weight over her
darkened mounds until it obscures her,
and only I know it hurts.

Today the love-vine
threatens Grandmother's only lemon tree,

five fruit since she planted it six years ago,
and now the invader will love it to death.

Mother yanks the vine out and finds
roots deeper than a mirror.

She ordered new gravel
for the driveway,
the three of us hauling off grey slate for black,
since both cars leak oil and we can't take them back.

Last night Grandmother dreamt of a runaway horse
galloping through dried corn, lost in the whispering ears.

    Corn for anonymity.

We look over our left shoulders at the new rising moon,
wish for health and wealth—

the moon winks back,
its shoulders edging the sky,

a brilliant wedge you could stick
your fingers into and pull the sky open,
easy as a birthday present.

We spend all night dreaming
on the back porch,

Orion hanging so huge
and low his staff pierces our roof,

his chapped lion skin robe hanging
darkness in sheets around us.

Poor blind and beautiful Orion, looking always west
where he'll never recover his sight—

he follows the moon higher,
growing vague

until his path is traced by Dawn,
who loves him so much she kills him.

We let the sun track us inside,
lay down together and breathe each other into sleep.

Day will fix everything not-dead.

Jupiter's in a triple with the moon tonight,
and Venus at dawn in the East—

Grandmother's praying to our shellacked Mary,
crowned princess, goddess in a thin blue shift,

while Mother paints her own breasts
gold with saffron paste,

needles the ends of fresh raw eggs
and blows the mess

over a cookie plate, reads devious
patterns in the yolks.

Grandmother can divine
with entrails,

though Mother banned her from it.
Who would eat a hen portending rain?

Mother hammers lead fishing weights into charms
against flamboyance.

The rain is so cruel, our chickens refuse
to stand face into the wind.

The postman won't come,
our box stands damp and empty,

save for the clunks of charcoal and talc
Mother placed inside for positive spirits and money.

Grandmother sits in her whalebone chair and curses the rain.
Mother hands us onions for increased appetite—

we've got more fowl
coming than Palestine had Canaanites,
one cock and brooders we can't even name.

We've eaten fertile eggs for days,
each closer and closer to chicken-ness,

a bent neck, a foot, a tiny stone eye scrambled
with peppers and beefsteak tomatoes ripened
along the neighbor-edge of our fence.

Venus reemerges at midnight.
Jupiter enters Pisces.

Sharp inter-egg cheeping from the coop.

Mother prognosticates dryness for tomorrow,
balls up a box of tin foil
and places the shining planet by the door.

Jupiter for weather changes, tin for luck.

Grandmother says a prayer
to St. Joseph of Arimathea,
the tinsmith, though we all know that saints
make less good for weather
than Samson made for the Philistines.

We dream of water: means *water*.

Our cock has gotten bold
and Grandmother's after it with a hoe.

She's sure he grew razors on his ankles
from hate and spite,

but Mother and I check the gate and we're right:
Someone's messing with our chickens.

The cock cackles around the saw palmetto
that bites at Grandmother's forearms

as she hacks over it with her rusty tool,
red berries flying like flak.

The cock settles high in our holly like Jupiter
in all his heavenly splendor

and Grandmother beneath him,
raging herself to ash.

During Grandmother's nap
Mother and I coax the cock

down with linguini and hard-boiled yolk
spiked with Mother's herbal opiate.

The cock finds himself some chicken sleep
and we cut the bands and razors from his feet.

His open eyes are dumb, round stones,
jasper inside sardonyx.

Mother dresses his ankles with salt and tea,
wraps them tight.

I know he's dreaming of chickens:
means worry or enemies planning against you.

His feathers feel like spring,
new and buttery,

the fingers
of his wrinkly crown

like a woman's inner foldings,
his hard beak split like a mussel.

It's like holding a miracle after the awe
has worn away,

the body of life and death, and I could
love him

to my breast or shatter
his head on the stones.

III

Extremely Lightweight Guns

I don't like makin' money, I just love sellin' guns
—Don, of Don's Guns

Literally no recoil, and if the steel is cold, I don't know it. If bullets taste like gardenias, like tongues, like bathwater or greasy fingers, wine floweth-ing over in my tin field cup, I don't know it. I don't like makin' money, I just love sellin' guns. I ache all day for a smoothbore shot; I'm a hammer-cocker, trigger-friendly, barrel-ready, slide that slide and make the sight sure. I want the longest operating rod you got. I want to stare down that dark pill, find my mark, carry the pheasant home. I have an ivory two-shot in my panties drawer, a loaded revolver under my downy pillow, and at the pawnshop, a rack fuller than a pinup calendar. I'll mail 'em unmarked if you ask. I got a modern Howitzer out back, you can rock that cradle for a couple bucks. But it's not the money. There's nothing sexier than the Bill of Rights. Well, maybe an old cannon with a full wad and a wooden rammer. How do bullets taste? Some say gardenias, tongues, bathwater, greasy fingers, deep red wine flowing over in your cup. A bullet's core snapping into point, your mother's sweet voice. The shot recoiling into your hands, the pitch in your legs after a father's belt. Pull it again. The real impact, again. I've got steel between my teeth. My dentist loves me. The neighbors hate me. I ask the guns every day, fuck me.

Here's a Pill

The night is a knife standing on end. There's a bird outside in the darkness, singing alone. If you don't like yourself, here's a pill. It's yellow, like the flowers planted outside the home you want to sell. There may be something left of your heart, that crazy midnight bird plotting against its cage. The night will be still. The trees will hang like treasonous soldiers. You can preserve the knife and let the bird exhaust the tree at 3:00 a.m., the astonished night like a dark pill in your empty gullet, or you can let your shrunken body free in the song where your pill self waits to be born.

~

There's a bird outside in the darkness singing alone beside your yellow flowers and nobody bought the house today. The pill you want to sell hangs in the bird's gullet like 3:00 a.m. If your heart is a knife, the song is a shrunken body towing you through the night like that crazy bird carrying your sleep in its hard cleft mouth. Nothing will be left of the house. The cage conspires against its bird. In another pill, a bird waits to be born. You can exit the house and free the bird. The new owners will want to know what pill whimpers there like a knife waiting for execution. If the flowers won't hawk the house, here's a pill.

~

Outside the name you want to sell, flowers perch like yellow gizzards. The yellow pill sings in the night, alone. The darkening house is what you call your body at 3:00 a.m. when the bird's mouth is a difficult shell and the house your only sharpened tool. If you can't find the bird, here's a pill. Here's a knife standing on end in the only house you recognize. The new owners will want to know why the pill sings and the bird doesn't. You will answer that the pill has shrunken the bird inside your gullet, where it contrives to keep sleep at knife's edge, the flowers in a porcelain bowl, and your name like the night ebbing from the bird's beak, waiting for the pill to sustain it.

The House That We Built

As if my fingers could cleave the brick,
    as if the brick wasn't stone, as if the stone

made whole the house whose empty rooms
    weigh time's disaster; make the stone,

cleave the brick, make and remake, remake;
    yes, wind; yes, water; the house persists.

As if my hands could brick the cleave
    threatening the house, as if those ruddy

stones were not placed by men, as if the stones
    weren't sometimes frail, as if the men

that made the house did not have hands
    to close the cleave and stack the brick—

darling, you're the house, or I'm the house.
    Or you're the stone that makes the brick

that firms the house and I'm the hands
    that try to cleave, or you're the fingers

that lay the brick that built the house,
    and I'm the cleave that your hands close.

PLANNED DISAPPEARANCES

On October 17th, Mars attains its brightest apparent magnitude
of this apparition, visible to the naked eye for the first time in
months in the Northern Hemisphere.
—Astronomy Essentials

Tonight Mars resurfaced, as if he was ever gone.
Tonight I had my glasses on.

I've missed bigger planets than that.
I bought cream today that wanted to be butter.

I ran out of soap. Killed a sow.
You can make butter from blood.

Lamentations: 4:3: *The daughter of my people*
is become cruel, like the ostriches in the wilderness.

If the bed ain't made for three, stretch it.
If the bed don't fit seven, make room on the floor.

Complaints will be tried with soap and blood.
Wash thyself and thy city. You're a filthy ostrich.

Lamentations: 4:5: *Those who ate dainties*
are deserted in the streets;

May we all rejoice under Mars 'cause soon he'll be gone.
That's how the sky works: Everyone gets a turn.
It's what's so great about the cosmos.

What did Jesus think, and did he have time,
between making birds from tough Israeli clay

and more-trout from some-trout to notice
Mars and his planned disappearances?

Typically insensitive of a planet like that.

Perhaps: *The red star is wandering again.*

Lamentations: 3:15: *He has filled me with bitterness;*
boil blood, fill intestines, salt, gristle, sand, teeth.

Coagulation is like opening the camera's shutter to the sky.

We have records of your movements.
When Mars screams, pretend you can't hear it.

There are six folks in my bed, a pig's head,
and everyone greasy with duck liver and eggs.
We're a sick little family, naked, rolling on crackers in our bed.

Give unto us ham hocks in jelly, sour green peppers
in Cajun sauce, okra and tomatoes,

let us be anointed with the fattest green dollar bills,
with Crisco and the light of living stars and cheap,

sweet port wine, for we have asked for nothing
and received much, for we have lain together with blood

and garbage under Mars who is just a red speck
you can wipe away like sneeze on a windshield.

THE INCUBATOR

Make them eggs.

I've tried to be a hen but
The egg wants more than mothering.
Or wants to be other than an egg—white stone, dark stone, wood.
Something more independent.

The hardest thing is departing an egg.
An egg is more miracle than its contents.
It knows nothing but the chipping-away.
If it wanted, it could be a bird.

The egg is more miracle than its contents.

The plain, understandable
yolk, the innocent albumen
giving way to a breather,
this hard womb.

This hard womb.

Three years into puberty, I wouldn't be pried open.
He chased me from his mother's house wielding that pink,
comfortable, Styrofoam tray in his pitching hand, each cold
ovum nestled inside.

I wouldn't be pried open.

Remember, after sex, in the pre-dawn we'd go to Denny's
in Little Haiti for coffee and eggs: Benedict,
scrambled, over easy, sunny side up. Sometimes, Sundays,
Little Havana, *chorizo* omelets.

Make it warm, clutch it in your hand.
Now imagine it's a candle. The closest you'll come to discarding life.

Even on the best of farms, the cock will find the hen.
The immature vein pretending gestation is easy.

Even on the best of farms, the cock will find the hen.

Fecund, suffering oval, spider's silk, knitting violence
into a snatch of wing, of nare. When the chick draws
down before pipping, when its egg tooth disregards
the sac, there's nothing like this desire, not even yours.

There's nothing like this desire.

It's an earnest gamete. It would love to please you. Boil broth, drop
it whisked by the teaspoon. Add salt. Sugar. Swear it's alive,
even though it lays there like a seed. Even dried corn,
made into a necklace, will grow.

Swear it's alive.

Choose your chickens wisely.
Hold your eggs lightly.
Place the duck's children in a shoebox beneath the furnace.
Someday, when you grow up, you'll pay for them by the pound.

By the pound.

A friend, a bodybuilder, eats twenty whites a day. His child
is friendly. He slips her the yolks.
Her cry is calcium.
The mother points—*What's this?* Nose, ears, mouth, vagina.

The child knows her yolks.
She grows. In nine months she'll be a womb.
The egg grows too.
If it were a baby, it would desire darkness.

It would desire darkness.

We cracked a double-yolker. If we lived in a village
in Eastern Europe three hundred years ago, we'd be witches.
Instead, in New York City, we proclaimed, *twins!* like with cherries
or Siamese tomatoes. It was no more magic than breakfast.

It was no more magic than breakfast.

At thirteen we broke eggs into mailboxes.
It was a federal crime.
We were incubators with raw felonies in our fists.
The mailboxes were incubators. The government was an incubator.

We were incubators.

All those eggs popping like blisters. That sonic crack shunting you out of sleep.
The egg speaks from the incubator like a real bird.
Have you heard it, the egg twisting itself into chickenhood?
Help it with a toothpick, it speaks to you forever.

A real bird.

Procreation is nothing more than math.
There are twelve eggs in the refrigerator.
One hundred million humans in ten grams of sperm. One egg a month.
That's omelets for three.

Omelets for three.

Hollow, cracked, in the damp willows, last year's nest
soaks in this year's flooding. Migration. How beautiful they were,
the blizzard-blue shoulders breaching brown feathers,
teenage mallards wading through reeds for our pizza crusts.

The neighbors shot a Muscovy hen as she paddled in their Jacuzzi.
Her nest, at my front door, never hatched.
The Jacuzzi was new.
The neighbors don't fuck around.

Hollow, cracked.

We're all eggs. Forget that, forget you breathe.
If you were wood, but you're not.
Even stones want to be warmed.
Hold them in your hands, too. Make them eggs.

IV

THE DRESSMAKER LOST IN HIS NEEDLES

after Larry Levis

Thread by thread the flax seed finds
    the sun above the marl

in a world that comes and goes in the torn
    fibers of its linens;

one by one the needles dull
    and multiply in their wooden box.

Fine points, fine eyes,
    fine silver poses of yearning.

The dressmaker's wife won't
    live out the year, her eyes

now something not part of herself,
    her legs stiff and false

as seed husks strewn
    to starving birds,

and the dressmaker must live on
    at the end of his bolts of cotton.

So too his wife with the clots in her brain,
    whose blood sleeps like a seed

thickening beneath July,
    won't live on through fall.

The wind startles the summer's heat,
    whistling through the breach

in the tiny stained glass window
       the dressmaker's wife pieced years ago

for the dressmaker's studio door.
       But the dressmaker isn't listening.

He knows that clothes and wind-song
       are delusions, that draping women

and the world are one, that wind
       and women both agree on nothing,

like the two halves of a brain gone muddy
       as the edge of a lake after storms.

The dressmaker thought
       the brain wasn't a concern

until he saw it this morning on the doctor's film,
       his wife's life spreading out in black

smudges, ten thousand crows in summer,
       each breaching

an artery, spilling her
       and laughing as they did it.

The dressmaker blinked his eyes and tried
       to will the doctor into another diagnosis.

To him, the doctor was an emperor
       bequeathing medicine

that kills the brain, pills
       like viper's eyes, toxic seeds.

Christmas lights glistened
        above the dressmaker like suns

in some laughing world,
        and because it was Christmas,

the doctor shook the dressmaker's hand
        slow as the weaving of a moth's cocoon

in the weeks before frost. His wife was still alive,
        still needing dressing and feeding, loving,

not the indifference of a thousand pills,
        a thousand eyeless needles.

A dressmaker for all these years,
        to have sewn for princesses and queens,

proper women, gaunt runway models
        whose clavicles felt like bird bones,

hollow and ordinary, rich women who preferred
        dyed feathers and golden ropes,

day after day in a world
        that comes and goes, laughing

as the idea of death burned like silk under a hot iron.
        He left his wife in the hospital then,

went to his studio, slept there and dreamed about a mouse
        he once trapped under his cutting table,

its head beneath stiff wire, not quite dead.
        He envisioned the mouse creeping around

at night, making a nest of pins
　　　　and threads, holing up the walls.

The way it drank cola from near empty cups,
　　　　dipping its head in like a bird,

washing its face with its paws. He told the mouse
　　　　it shouldn't have eaten through his bolt

of white eyelet, the black cotton jersey,
　　　　or chewed a thousand holes

in the rayon and silk. There it lay, whiskers
　　　　twitching like silver threads, consumer of hundreds

of dollars of fabric, two months rent, at least.
　　　　Then Pearl, his old seamstress, comes in

with an irredeemable oil stain on a silk gown,
　　　　crying like someone who has just lost a son,

and the dressmaker gives her an hour off
　　　　and ten dollars and she goes

to the cafeteria next door for a milkshake.
　　　　He scrubs the oil stain in the sink, and then Pearl

runs back inside, looking crazed, tearing the silk gown
　　　　from his hands and putting it on

over her own tight skirt and cheap red rayon blouse,
　　　　her anger strange in the calm studio,

a rage he didn't recognize. All he wanted was the dress back,
　　　　and to go home, remembering when the woman

he loved wore silk gowns herself,
        before her brain wasn't ink on a notepad,

a million crows taking a wheat field by force.
        He'd told his wife that no one could die in a silk gown,

the dress he sewed from lies with a pattern he stole
        from other husbands, other wives.

He'd wanted her to smile then, but her face was a husk
        incapable of refilling itself.

"Pearl," he said, as his seamstress swiped
        at the growing stain,

"I killed a mouse today. It's in the dumpster."
        She turned on him then with his shears in her hand,

the shears she's never allowed to touch,
        the shears his mother gave him after the war,

the shears he sharpened after each dress, the shears
        he didn't recognize as his own in Pearl's thin hands,

her screaming growing louder, the edge of the dress
        tearing under her feet.

He lay on the floor covered with the silk gown,
        a blanket beneath which is a darkness that pleases

him for a moment, like a dress pattern that comes
        to him in a dream.

He removes the torn shroud from over
        his body and begins to sew it into a cape

for which he will charge half what the fabric costs.
        The brain bleeds memory without the dignity of choice.

The indignity of blood swirling into cavities in the head,
        crows, mice. It's quiet enough to hear his fabrics

rustle on their own, wanting the sun again, perhaps the worm,
        or water. Fabric doesn't die.

But people do. Stroke is a word he didn't like.
        Stroke. Like the crayon marks on an unsewn dress.

Then his wife is standing naked next to him. He imagines
        a dress for her. He sews it for more than an hour.

He can't see her, but he knows she's there.
        It's more than the fabric whispering,

the light of the afternoon blue through the tiny glass window,
        and the wind whispering too, soon the mice

in the walls whispering until the city darkens,
        but he keeps listening, sewing,

crying now because he finally understands,
        and he's stuck by a pin left in the fabric.

The dressmaker feels foolish for not having taken it out
        as habit, but even as he pulls it out, another appears.

He throws the gown against the wall, shattering a photo
        of his wife, but when he looks up, nothing has happened,

the photo on the wall gleaming in the sodium light from outside,
        so unsettled it may have well been nothing

more than a signal all those years. The whispering
    calls to him now, clear as that yellow light,

and he turns to his studio and says to no one
    and to everyone together: "Take this fabric,

these tortoise shell buttons, zippers and thread,
    and make your own damn dresses."

He sweeps the floor of pins as he always has,
    then walks out with his wife into the darkness,

which is not a city at all, but a giant seed whose husk
    glows and sings. He sees Pearl bending over his body,

still wearing the silk gown, shears limp in her hand,
    crying, tearing at the stained dress.

She has taken the wheat field by force.
    The wind outside weeps.

Then he realizes that he's the wind.
    He turns back, and though she can't hear him,

he tells Pearl to remember to set the iron on low
    for synthetics, to chalk the fabric before she cuts,

but he hears how absurd his voice sounds,
    not a thing for council anymore,

but something to push through a crack
    in a stained glass window.

He once mentioned to Pearl that he should putty that crack,
    but she didn't even look up from her hemming.

And the mouse in the dumpster?
    It's wind too, pausing inside the house

like a photo on the wall, waiting like memory
    for someone to whisk open the door.

Biographical Note

Nikki Moustaki is the recipient of a National Endowment for the Arts grant in poetry and the author of *The Bird Market of Paris: A Memoir* and *The Complete Idiot's Guide to Writing Poetry*. She has written for *Good Housekeeping*, the *New York Times*, *Publishers Weekly*, the *Miami Herald*, and the *Village Voice*, among others. She holds an MA in poetry from New York University, an MFA in poetry from Indiana University, and an MFA in fiction from New York University. Her poetry, fiction, and essays have appeared in various literary magazines, anthologies, and college textbooks. She splits her time between Miami Beach and New York City.